Setting and Using Criteria
Second Edition

By Kathleen Gregory, Caren Cameron, Anne Davies

A Joint Publication

Solution Tree

Connections
Publishing

Published in the US by Solution Tree Press
555 North Morton Street
Bloomington, IN 47404
800.733.6786 (toll free) / 812.336.7700
FAX: 812.336.7790

email: info@solution-tree.com
solution-tree.com

Printed in the United States of America

15 14 13 12 11   1 2 3 4 5

FSC
Mixed Sources
Product group from well-managed
forests and other controlled sources
Cert no. SW-COC-002283
www.fsc.org
© 1996 Forest Stewardship Council

Library of Congress Cataloging-in-Publication Data

Gregory, Kathleen.
  Setting and using criteria / by Kathleen Gregory, Caren Cameron, Anne
Davies. – 2nd ed.
    p. cm. – (Knowing what counts)
    ISBN 978-1-935543-73-2 (perfect bound) – ISBN 978-1-935543-74-9
(library edition)
  1. Curriculum-based assessment. 2. Interdisciplinary approach in education. 3. Education–Standards. 4. Grading and marking (Students) I.
Cameron, Caren. II. Davies, Anne. III. Title.
  LB3060.32.C74G74 2011
  371.27′2–dc22
                                    2011008106

Solution Tree
Jeffrey C. Jones, CEO & President

Solution Tree Press
President: Douglas M. Rife
Publisher: Robert D. Clouse
Vice President of Production: Gretchen Knapp
Managing Production Editor: Caroline Wise
Senior Production Editor: Risë Koben

Connections Publishing
Stewart Duncan, CEO & President
Project Manager: Judith Hall-Patch
Design: Mackenzie Duncan, Kelly Giordano, Cori Jones, Pat Stanton

Acknowledgments

We would like to thank all the students, parents, and educators with whom we have worked. Also, we would like to thank Annalee Greenberg, our editor at A. Greenberg and Associates, for posing thoughtful questions and offering insights.

—Kathleen Gregory, Caren Cameron,
and Anne Davies

Contents

3. Questions and Responses   57

What happens to grades when we use these
approaches?/**57**   How did our record keeping change when we used criteria?/**60**
Can students use these approaches for self-
assessment?/**62**   What about the students
who cannot meet all the criteria?/**63**   How can
I convince my students that they can live without grades?/**63**

Foreword

Middle school teacher Barb Boerchers recently asked her class the following question: "Let's say you didn't have criteria; you didn't know how you were being assessed. You just received feedback or a mark. Think about that. How would you feel, and why would you feel that way?"

Three students, all male, immediately put up their hands and responded:

> Student 1—"I would feel disappointed because I didn't get a criteria sheet and I would have done much better cuz [sic] maybe I missed out on a punctuation but if I wanted to look at the criteria I'd probably want to scan the story or whatever for punctuation."

> Student 2—"Well, I would feel kind of disappointed because I know I could have done better because I could have known what I was being assessed on."

> Student 3—"Probably most of the mistakes would have been stupid mistakes that I should have fixed and that I should have had right if I'd had the criteria. That would just make me feel very frustrated."

As we listen to this feedback from eighth-grade learners, they remind us, in their own words, of what Rick Stiggins states: "Students can reach any target that they know about and holds still for them." When teachers work not only to share the learning destination with their students, but to identify what quality evidence of learning looks like en route to the learning destination, then students have a much clearer picture of what they need to know, do, and articulate.

Consider this scenario:
A teacher returns a grade-ten science lab report to a student. She tells the student, "You can do better than this. If you just pull up your socks and try harder, the lab report will improve in its content and format." The teacher states that the student can re-do the work and submit it in the next couple of days to be reassessed. And then, the teacher walks away.

If that student is a "good" student and has come to understand what the teacher wants—through observation, inference, or memory—then she can do what needs to be done. However, if that student does not understand what the teacher wants in a science lab report, she is left to wonder what to do next to improve it. She may attempt it a second time; she may change a section or a statement that was already correct; she may ask the teacher or her peers for help; she may make some random changes and hope for the best; or she may simply give up.

Let's replay that scenario:
A teacher returns a grade-ten science lab report to a student. She tells the student that she has added some written feedback based on the criteria that are posted on the wall describing what makes up a quality science lab report in this classroom. In fact, a copy is attached to the student's work. Areas from the criteria that have "not yet been met" are highlighted. The teacher states that the student can re-do the work and submit it in the next couple of days to be reassessed. And then, the teacher walks away.

In this case, the student has specific and descriptive feedback against the criteria that she has come to understand deeply. In fact, the student was part of co-constructing those very criteria several weeks ago. She recalls how the teacher distributed samples of what she considered to be quality science lab reports. The class discussed the elements of those reports and built criteria around it. Based on the feedback, the student can more confidently make changes to her report. She knows what needs to be changed and what can stay the same.

In *Testing, Motivation and Learning*, Harlen and Deakin Crick (2002) of the Assessment Reform Group state that teachers need to involve students more often in setting criteria and assessing themselves against those criteria. This strategy becomes powerful and possible to do using the four-step process found in *Setting and Using Criteria*.

Since the first edition of this book appeared in 1997, teachers have made the four-step process their own. Some teachers give students sticky notes to write down their brainstormed ideas. They move the sticky notes around to sort their ideas and then determine a category or criterion that best represents the details. Other teachers have students write down an idea on a long strip of paper. Students then gather into groups, talking and determining the sorting criteria as they move around the room. And still other teachers use electronic whiteboards to manipulate a list of brainstormed ideas into groupings that the class agrees upon. The possibilities are endless.

For many, the term *co-construction of criteria* has become the norm. It is something done together, as all learners in the community work alongside each other. When a critical detail is omitted while a list is brainstormed, the teacher, as a member of that community, adds his idea. This is not manipulation of the process, but rather a moment that provides evidence of authentic group learning.

Kathleen, Caren, and Anne have set out, in both accessible and invitational language, not only the four-step process, but also the answer to "What next?" That is, once criteria have been set, how can teachers, students, and others use it to provide specific and descriptive feedback to self and others?

The second part of this book offers ten ways to provide feedback without assigning a mark. Since *Setting and Using Criteria* was first published, three major research reports have affirmed the importance of specific, descriptive feedback without marks (Black & Wiliam, 1998; Hattie & Timperley, 2007; Shute, 2008). Research also reports that marks, grades, or general praise interfere with learning; this is particularly true for those students who tend to fail in classroom situations.

Black and Wiliam (1998) state that specific, descriptive feedback is essential to learning, yet there never is enough time for a teacher to give adequate feedback to students. Again, students need to be partners in the process. As teachers model how to use these ten strategies, students can engage in providing feedback to themselves and to others. In this way, feedback increases using the shared language of assessment. As criteria are used to anchor these conversations, everyone is clear about what quality is and about what is expected. What once may have been the sole property of the teacher is now made public and clear.

Quality classroom assessment has the largest positive impact on student learning and achievement ever documented (Crooks, 1988; Black & William, 1998; Meisels et al., 2003; Rodriguez, 2004). Co-construction of criteria and its use by students and teachers is a part of that picture. Perhaps more importantly, it provides students with voice and opportunity. Their voice is added to that of the teacher to talk about what is important in the learning process and product. As well, students develop a vocabulary of assessment in order to communicate their learning to others.

These same researchers have determined that the positive impact on student learning and achievement is especially true for those students who struggle the most. How true this is. Reflect on the difference between the two scenarios on page 8. For the student who struggled to intuit what the teacher wanted in the lab assignment, the criteria for success were much clearer in the second case.

Let us go back to where we began—in the classroom. Barb Boerchers, the middle years teacher, explains it in this way: "By sharing the [process of setting] criteria with the students . . . they are engaged in their learning . . . it makes sense. [The student] knows this is what I have to do, this is why I have to do it and this is the strategy to get it done. And that's the whole thing—setting the floor so they can communicate."

Sandra Herbst
Assistant Superintendent of Schools
Winnipeg, Manitoba

References

Black, P. & D. Wiliam. (1998). Inside the black box: Raising standards through classroom assessment. *Phi Delta Kappan, 80*(2), 1–20.

Crooks, T. (1988). The impact of classroom evaluation on students. *Review of Educational Research, 58*(4), 438–481.

Harlen, W. & R. Deakin Crick. (2002). *Testing, Motivation and Learning*. Booklet produced by Assessment Reform Group at University of Cambridge Faculty of Education.

Hattie, J. & H. Timperley. (2007). The power of feedback. *Review of Educational Research, 77*(1), 81–112.

Meisels, S., S. Atkins-Burnett, Y. Xue, & D. Bickel. (2003). Creating a system of accountability: The impact of instructional assessment on elementary children's achievement scores. *Educational Policy Analysis Archives, 11*(9), 19 pgs. Downloaded from http://epaa.asu.edu/epaa/v11n9/ on September 19, 2004.

Rodriguez, M. C. (2004). The role of classroom assessment in student performance on TIMSS. *Applied Measurement in Education, 17*(1), 1–24.

Shute, V. J. (2008). Focus on formative feedback. *Review of Educational Research, 78*(1), 153–189.

1. Setting Criteria

What are criteria, and why do we set them?

Criteria are, simply, the standards by which something can be judged or valued. When we determine these criteria, we are deciding what counts.

Teachers can set criteria *for* their students. Teachers can set criteria *with* their students. Students can set or negotiate their own criteria. In this book, we show many ways to involve students in setting criteria. That's because we have found that when students take part in developing criteria, they are much more likely to understand what is expected of them, "buy in," and then accomplish the task successfully.

In our classrooms, we usually set criteria for projects and assignments with our students. We do not set criteria for everything, nor should we.

We regularly remind ourselves of the purpose of using criteria by asking the question, "How is this supporting student learning?"

A four-step process for setting criteria with students

We have found that the following four-step process

for setting criteria with students encourages student participation, understanding, and ownership:

Step one. Brainstorm.

Step two. Sort and categorize.

Step three. Make and post a T-chart.

Step four. Add, revise, refine.

The first three steps of the process are carried out either before or as students are beginning their projects and assignments. It's important to set criteria before beginning the assignment or during the planning stages.

STEP ONE: BRAINSTORM

Teachers and students already have criteria in their heads. Getting everyone's ideas, including the teacher's, out in the open helps to build ownership and develop a common understanding of what is expected.

1. Pose a question such as "What counts in a lab report?" "What am I looking for when I grade your paragraphs?" or "What counts in an oral presentation?"

<u>What counts in an oral presentation?</u>

- look up and look at your audience
- have to be able to hear you
- no fidgeting
- look interested
- use small cards for notes
- make it interesting by using pictures or diagrams
- use lots of expression
- slow down
- stand straight
- keep it short
- use specific examples to get your point across
- make sure you have a conclusion
- we need to know what your topic is right away

Teacher input

Figure 1: Brainstormed list

2. Record all ideas, in students' words, on chart paper.

3. Contribute your own ideas. Students will often focus on surface features, so teachers need to ensure the essential features of the project are included and the standards or outcomes of the subject area are reflected in the criteria for the student work (see figure 1 above).

It looks like we've got a number of ideas that are about being <u>interesting to an audience</u>. Let's code those ideas with / .

We've also said a lot about making a presentation <u>easy to follow</u>. Let's code those ideas with F .

When we look at the ideas we have left, it seems that they're mainly about your <u>speech and manner</u>. Let's code those ideas with S .

What counts in an oral presentation?

S - look up and look at your audience

S - have to be able to hear you

S - no fidgeting

/ - look interested

F - use small cards for notes

/ - make it interesting by using pictures or diagrams

S - use lots of expression

F - slow down

S - stand straight

/ - keep it short

F - use specific examples to get your point across

F - make sure you have a conclusion

F - we need to know what your topic is right away

Figure 2: Coded list

STEP TWO: SORT AND CATEGORIZE

To help students remember criteria, we limit the number to what the brain can remember (usually three to five). It is also important to use language and terms that students understand.

1. Ask students to look at the brainstormed list to find any ideas that fit together. Ask questions such as "Do you see any patterns where certain ideas fit together?" or "I see a number of ideas that are about accuracy; can you find any ideas that fit under this heading?" Other possible questions include "Does it make sense to put these ideas under this heading?" "Are there any ideas that fit here, too?" or "Is there a big idea or heading that would capture these points?"

2. Show how the ideas fit together by using different colored pens to code them. In one color, circle ideas that are related. You can also use symbols to represent the "big ideas" and label the idea with the appropriate symbol (see figure 2).

3. Talk to students about how similar ideas can fit under different headings. Tell them that by grouping similar ideas together we have a more manageable number to work with.

Criteria
for oral presentations

Details / Specifics

- interesting to an audience
  - look interested in your subject
  - make it interesting
  - keep it short

- easy to follow
  - use small cards for notes
  - slow down
  - use specific examples to get your point across
  - make sure you have a conclusion
  - we need to know what your topic is right away

- speech and manner help the audience listen
  - look up and look at your audience
  - have to be able to hear you
  - no fidgeting
  - stand straight
  - use lots of expression

Figure 3: T-chart

STEP THREE: MAKE AND POST A T-CHART

Posting a visual reminder of the criteria (what counts), along with the details of specific criteria (what you'll be looking for), reminds students exactly what they are working toward and what they need to do to get there.

1. Draw a large T-chart, such as the one in figure 3, on chart paper.

2. Label the big ideas, or categories, from the brainstormed list. These are the criteria.

3. Transfer these onto the left-hand side of the T-chart.

4. Put the specific ideas from the brainstormed list on the right-hand side of the T-chart, opposite the criteria they fit in. Ask: "Do you need any more ideas or details to understand any of the criteria?"

5. Post the T-chart and ask: "What else could help you remember the criteria?" (For example, "Copy them into your notebook.")

STEP FOUR: ADD, REVISE, REFINE

Developing criteria is never finished—we re-examine, add, change, and delete throughout the year.

1. Have students review the criteria periodically. After completing an assignment or after learning a new skill, ask students: "Are there any new criteria we need to add? Is there anything we've listed that someone doesn't understand? Have we included any criteria that are not significant?"

2. Make any changes on the chart, and date the changes as a reminder that setting criteria is an ongoing process (see figure 4, opposite).

Scenarios for setting criteria with students

Following are five different scenarios for setting criteria with students. Although originally designed for specific subject areas, they are easily transferable to other curricular areas. Find the one(s) that best fit you, your students, and your subject area.

USING PERSONAL EXPERIENCE

One way to introduce the concept of criteria is to start with something that all students understand—and that has meaning for them. One teacher, who had never used criteria with her grade-seven students, started by developing criteria

Criteria for oral presentations	Details / Specifics

- interesting to an
  audience
	- look interested in your subject
	- make it interesting
	- keep it short
	- use your own experiences (Oct.)
	- involve the audience by asking a
	  question (Oct.)

- easy to follow	- use small cards for notes
	- slow down
	- use specific examples to get your
	  point across
	- make sure you have a conclusion
	- we need to know what your topic
	  is right away

- speech and manner
  helps the audience
  listen
	- look up and look at your audience
	- have to be able to hear you
	- no fidgeting
	- stand straight
	- use lots of expression
	- no monotone (Oct.)

Figure 4: T-chart, revised

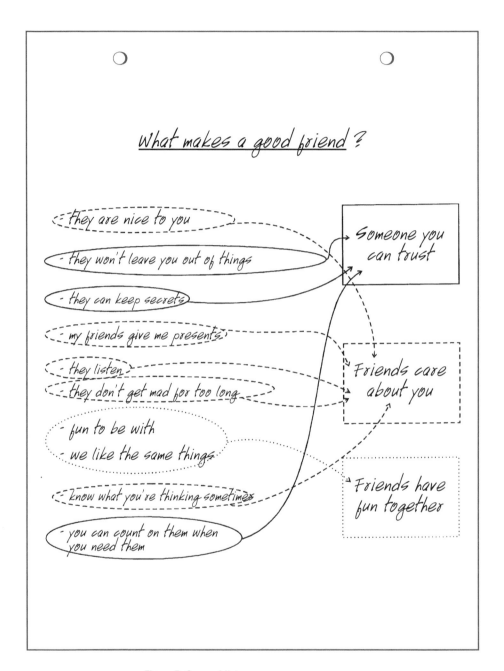

Figure 5: Grouped list

for a topic that was connected to students' personal experiences—what makes a good friend? They later were able to apply the process to their school assignments.

1. Ask students: "What makes a good friend?"

2. Ask students to each take two to three minutes to list all the qualities they can think of that make a good friend.

3. Have students turn to a partner, read their lists, and circle any common ideas that they recorded.

4. Meet as a whole class, and ask each pair of students to tell one idea from their shared list without repeating what someone else has said. Record these on the board or chart paper.

5. Continue to record ideas until students have run out of them.

6. Show the students how many of their ideas could fit together by grouping any that are similar. Give each group of ideas a category heading or title (see figure 5).

7. Ask students to write about what kind of a friend they are, based on the criteria.

USING FAMILIAR CLASSROOM EXPERIENCES

Students need to know enough about a learning experience to be able to develop criteria, so it is important to use familiar classroom experiences. One social studies teacher starts setting criteria with his grade-nine students by recalling a familiar assignment that they had done in past years—drawing a map.

Figure 6: a) Class brainstorm; b) Group sort and categorize; c) T-chart for map

1. Remind students that they have made maps many times before.

2. Ask students to brainstorm answers to the question "What counts when you draw a map?"

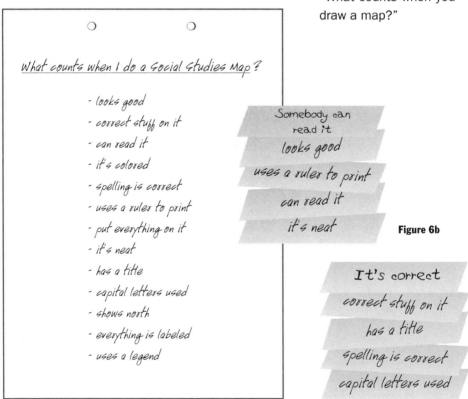

What counts when I do a Social Studies Map ?

- looks good
- correct stuff on it
- can read it
- it's colored
- spelling is correct
- uses a ruler to print
- put everything on it
- it's neat
- has a title
- capital letters used
- shows north
- everything is labeled
- uses a legend

Somebody can read it
looks good
uses a ruler to print
can read it
it's neat

Figure 6b

It's correct
correct stuff on it
has a title
spelling is correct
capital letters used

Figure 6a

3. Record their ideas on chart paper (see figure 6a). Contribute any essential ideas that students might miss, such as, "Use a legend or key."

4. Transfer the ideas from the chart paper onto a single sheet of paper. Make one copy for each group of three to four students.

5. The next day, give one copy to each group of three to four students.

(continued)

Criteria for Map	Details/Specifics
- easy to read and follow	- looks good - can read it - uses a ruler to print - it's neat
- labeling is accurate	- correct stuff on it - has title - capital letters used - spelling is correct
- map is complete	- it's colored - put everything on it - shows north - uses a legend - everything is labeled

Everything's done
it's colored
put everything on it
shows north
uses a legend
everything is labeled

Figure 6c

6. Have students cut the sheet into strips of individual ideas.

7. Ask students to sort and categorize the idea strips by putting them into three to five piles. Have them name each pile (see figure 6b on page 24).

8. Have students share with the whole class how they categorized the strips. Discuss the different ideas that groups came up with.

9. As a class, decide on the category names that will be used. Make a chart of the criteria (see figure 6c on page 25).

USING SPECIFIC EXAMPLES

One teacher shows his grade-eleven students how to set criteria for lab reports by using anonymous examples (science lab reports that students had done in previous years). By having actual examples before them, the students can see and describe the important and common features (see figure 7).

1. Give each group of three students copies of two or three different lab reports. Tell them that these are all good examples of work that students did last year, and you want them to examine these examples before they do any reports this year.

2. Ask each group to make a list of the important features that are common to the sample lab reports.

3. Have students post their lists for others to see.

4. Record on chart paper the features that the students found in the examples.

5. Group or web three to five similar ideas.

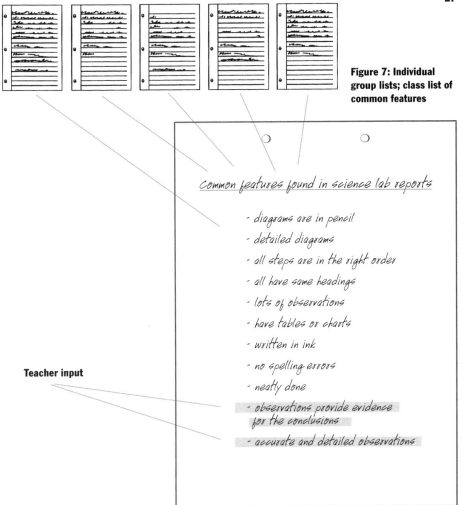

Figure 7: Individual group lists; class list of common features

Teacher input

Common features found in science lab reports

- diagrams are in pencil
- detailed diagrams
- all steps are in the right order
- all have same headings
- lots of observations
- have tables or charts
- written in ink
- no spelling errors
- neatly done
- observations provide evidence for the conclusions
- accurate and detailed observations

6. Ask students to name each group or web.

7. Post and talk about the groups (criteria), and add any essentials that may have been missed by the students, such as, "The observations provide evidence for the conclusion."

8. At the next class, give students an example of a lab report that does not meet all of the criteria. Ask: "What would a person need to do to make this lab report meet all the criteria?"

What you are supposed to learn in
this unit on solving problems:

- learn to identify and describe a problem
- select and use different strategies
- develop a plan to solve the problem
- see patterns and connections between problems
- reach a correct solution, knowing there may be more than one
- be willing to try again when the first way does not work out
- tell someone what you did to solve the problem
- say how the problem connects with something outside the classroom

Figure 8a

Figure 8: a) List of math standards or outcomes; b) T-chart

STARTING WITH STANDARDS OR OUTCOMES

A grade-eight math teacher sets criteria with students by telling the class what they are expected to learn in the unit. By using the standards as a starting point, she reinforces the link between the standards or outcomes and criteria for evidence of learning.

1. Post a list of math standards or outcomes in student-friendly language (see figure 8a, left). Tell students: "This is what you need to learn in this unit to solve problems in math."

2. Work with the class to answer the question "What does it look like and sound like when you've learned to problem-solve?" Pose specific questions that relate to each standard or outcome, such as "What are some of the strategies you use when you solve problems?" "How can you show that you are willing to try something again?" "What do you do to make sure that your solution is correct?" "How do you know if a problem has incomplete information?" and "How do you know what other information you need to solve such a problem?"

3. Record their responses on chart paper.

4. Refer to the original list of standards or outcomes. Ask: "Have we missed anything?" Work together to ensure that there are specifics and details for each of the standards or outcomes.

5. Sort and categorize the master list of ideas under three to five headings. Transfer to a T-chart (see figure 8b, below).

6. Start work on problem solving, using the T-chart as a guide.

Criteria for problem solving	Details / Specifics
- understand the problem	- can tell all parts of the problem - know what to do - can tell if a part is missing
- choose a strategy to solve it	- use diagrams to figure it out - think of similar problems that you've worked on - try different ways until it works
- tell about how you reached the solution	- break down the process into steps - check work
- give examples from outside the classroom	- we use the same math when buying carpet for our house

Figure 8b

BEGINNING WITH STUDENTS' IDEAS

When students have a choice in how they will represent their learning—a research paper, video presentation, or diorama, for example—it does not mean that there are different criteria for each type of representation. One student summed it up, asking, "How can you grade our work when we are all doing different things?" One grade-eight social studies teacher worked with the class to set criteria that would apply to the many ways they chose to show their learning. She began by having students think carefully about the projects on medieval times that they had just begun to research.

1. Ask students: "What would you like me to notice in the projects that you have been working on?" Give students two to three minutes to record three to five ideas.

2. Have students share their list with a partner and circle any common features.

3. On a chart, transcribe the list of common features from all the partners (see figure 9a, opposite).

4. In the next class, sort these features into broad categories. At this point, add in any other essential features that are missing.

5. Transfer to a T-chart. Post the chart (see figure 9b on page 32).

6. Pose the questions: "Can you see how the criteria fit with the way you have selected to represent your learning? Is there anything that we have left out?"

Figure 9a: List of criteria for research projects

What would you like me to notice in the project you have been working on?

- effort — time taken to do it
- clear and easy to read
- detail and information
- creativity
- presentation
- accuracy
- layout
- based on real events
- have a research question and answer it
- personal understanding
- creativity — original ideas
- organization
- neatness
- easy to read
- not boring
- design
- detailed characters
- facts / information
- realistic model or games — reflect Medieval Times
- good vocabulary — fits the times
- presentation

Criteria for project on
Medieval Times

Details / Specifics

Pose and answer a research question
- have a research question and answer it
- use accurate facts and information
- select key facts
- use a variety of sources

Summarize information showing personal learning and understanding
- work is detailed, informative, and factual
- organized clearly
- based on real events of the Middle Ages
- use historically correct vocabulary and concepts
- cite sources for your information

Communicate what you have learned through a choice of representation
- shows effort, time taken to do it
- make clear and easy to read
- make neat
- make it interesting
- reflect Medieval times with realistic model or game
- shows creativity
- has original ideas
- the representation format that you selected is appropriate to the subject matter and the sharing format

Teacher input

Figure 9b: T-chart

Setting criteria with students is only the beginning. To keep students focused on their learning, it is essential to link assessment practices to the established criteria.

2. Assessing Student Work in Relation to Criteria

What is assessment?

Assessment can be defined as the process of collecting data on student performance. This process includes observing students, talking and listening to students, and looking at students' work—such as projects, tests, and assignments.

We want to emphasize the distinction between assessment and evaluation. Assessment involves appraising a student's work and collecting selected work samples that clearly reflect that student's learning. Evaluation involves judging and interpreting the information from this data and, if required, assigning letter grades.

We have found that by placing more emphasis and spending more time on assessing students in a variety of ways, we increase the depth and accuracy of our evaluations. We remind ourselves that assessment (collecting data) is ongoing from the day that students enter our classroom, and that end-of-term evaluation for report cards (making judgments on that data) takes place three or four times a year.

As soon as we started assessing students in a variety of ways (and on an ongoing basis) we had to change the way we kept our grades. They no longer contain only scores. To capture the richness, variety, and depth of the assessments, our records now include criterion-based assessments, such as scaled scores, notes and observations, and self-assessments, as well as test scores and grades for assignments. The grades we assign need to reflect this increased depth of information about the student's learning. See further discussion in chapter 3, pages 57–61.

Shifting to criterion-based assessment

Once criteria have been set with students, teachers need to determine how student performance will be assessed in relation to those criteria. In this section, we offer ten ways to assess student work that don't involve giving grades, scores, percentages, or numbers. This helps students focus on the criteria that count.

Our move away from grading papers or projects is deliberate. When we started using criteria, we expected our students to focus on them. But when they got their papers back, they would look only at their score—not at the criteria and the learning these represented.

As teachers, we had shifted from comparing student work to looking at it in relation to the criteria. Our students had not.

To help our students make this shift, we developed ten ways to assess student work without putting a grade on the paper. We then used these assessment approaches on projects for which we and our students had set criteria. We found that when we assessed student work by not using the numbers and symbols associated with ranking and sorting, students began to focus on what really counts: what they are learning and what they can do to improve.

This does not mean that we never give grades to our students. They receive grades on tests, quizzes, right-and-wrong questions, and assignments for which we've not set criteria. All assessments, both qualitative and quantitative, are recorded. These provide the basis on which we evaluate student performance. We remind ourselves that we do not need to give a grade every time we assess student work; every day is not report card day. As teachers, we *do* need to make judgments about student performance in relation to criteria for reporting. We do this about three or four times a year—once we have assembled a representative assessment base.

Setting criteria with students and assessing their performance in relation to the criteria (and without grades) are ways to help students move beyond their focus on the grade or number ("What did I get?" "What's it worth?" "What do I need to do for an A?") and to concentrate on their learning ("This is what I'm doing well." "I need to improve in these areas." "The next thing I need to work on is. . ."). In this way, we use criteria to support the learning of all students.

Ten ways to assess without grading student work

We developed the following approaches with our students, and we encourage you to adapt them, not adopt them. Try those approaches that appeal to you, and discover those that work best with a particular project or assignment, with a particular group of students, or at a particular time of year.

We use a variety of assessment sheets, based on the sample at right, when assessing student work. These provide students with specific feedback about their work, and over time, give them a profile of their progress. Before we share our assessments with our students, we record the results. This gives us a wide range of assessment data on which to base our later evaluations.

Figure 10: Sample assessment sheet

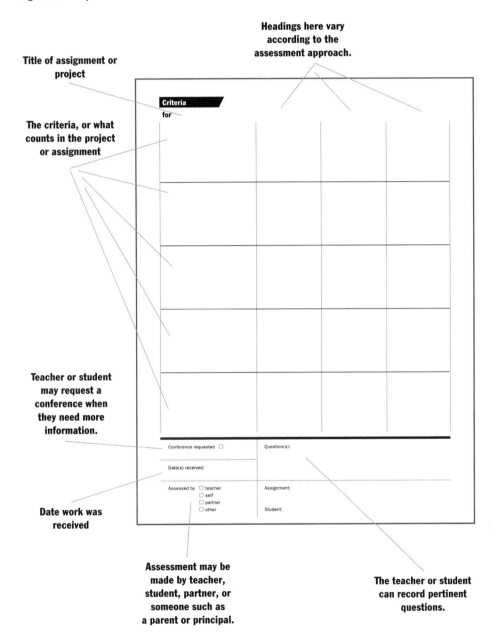

Headings here vary
according to the
assessment approach.

Title of assignment or
project

The criteria, or what
counts in the project
or assignment

Teacher or student
may request a
conference when
they need more
information.

Date work was
received

Criteria
for

Conference requested ☐

Date(s) received:

Assessed by ☐ teacher
☐ self
☐ partner
☐ other

Question(s):

Assignment:

Student:

Assessment may be
made by teacher,
student, partner, or
someone such as
a parent or principal.

The teacher or student
can record pertinent
questions.

Criteria		
for *reader response journal*	**Met**	**Not yet met**
- *recorded a minimum of 3 responses this week*		✓
- *included personal connections questions and predictions*	✓	
- *used the format we set up in class (re: headings, page numbers)*		✓

Conference requested ☐

Question(s):

Date(s) received: *Nov. 20*

Assessed by ☑ teacher
☐ self
☐ partner
☐ other

Assignment:
Reader Response

Student:
Andrew J., Block 3

Figure 11 : Met, Not yet met

MET, NOT YET MET

With this approach, the focus is on having students complete their work. This first step in using criteria separates what students are expected to complete from how well they complete it.

1. Set the criteria for a project. Teachers may set the criteria or refer to the four-step process (pages 13–20) for ways to involve students in doing this.

2. Make an assessment sheet such as the one illustrated at left for each student (or copy the reproducible in the appendix, page 69).

3. Assess student performance in relation to the criteria by putting a check mark (✓) in the "Met" or "Not yet met" column for each criteria statement.

4. Highlight those criteria that have not been met.

5. After giving assessment sheets to students, invite those who received *NY* to complete their work and resubmit it for reassessment.

6. Record student performance as *M* or *NY*. If students resubmit their work, record *R* for "Revised," adding an *M* if they then meet the criteria.

MET, NOT YET MET, I NOTICED

With this approach we move beyond completing work and focus on aspects of quality and/or progress in the work.

1. Set the criteria for a project. Teachers may set the criteria or refer to the four-step process for ways to involve students in doing this.

2. Make an assessment sheet, such as the one illustrated opposite, for each student (or copy the reproducible in the appendix, page 70).

3. Assess student performance in relation to the criteria by checking (✓) "Not yet met" and highlighting the material that needs attention, or checking (✓) "Met" and writing brief comments in the "I noticed . . ." column. These comments should focus on the quality of the work done and/or progress made since the last assignment.

4. Before giving assessment sheets to students, record student performance using *NY* or *M*. An asterisk can be used beside the *M* to indicate quality or specific progress.

5. If students resubmit their work, record *R* for "Revised," adding an *M* for "Met" if they then meet the criteria.

Figure 12: Met, Not yet met, I noticed

Criteria for *reader response journal*	Met	Not yet met	I noticed ...
- recorded a minimum of 3 responses this week	✓		you did 5 this week
- included personal connections questions and predictions	✓		you clearly express your feelings about the characters
- used the format we set up in class (re: headings, page numbers)		✓	

Conference requested ☐   Question(s):

Date(s) received: *Sept. 29*

Assessed by ☑ teacher
      ☐ self
      ☐ partner
      ☐ other

Assignment:
Reader Response

Student:
Sam T., Block A

SAMPLE MATCH

Many students need to both hear and see what it is that is expected of them. By showing students actual samples of work that meet criteria, then reviewing them together, students gain a clearer understanding of what counts.

1. Find two or three samples of a completed assignment or project that range from satisfactory to strong.

2. On the samples, write specific phrases, using the vocabulary of the criteria to point out aspects of the work

Figure 13: a) Sample; b) Sample match assessment sheet

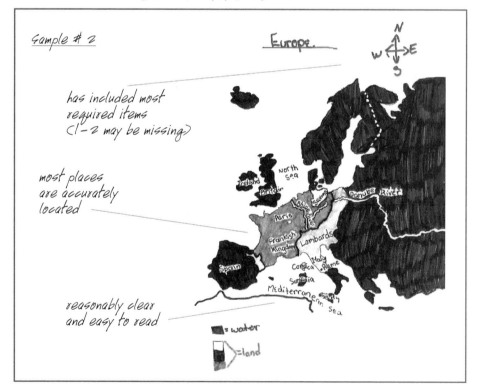

Figure 13a

that meet the criteria. These statements are descriptive and nonjudgmental (see figure 13a).

3. Number the samples, then post them for students to see.

4. Make an assessment sheet, such as the one illustrated below, for each student (or copy the reproducible in the appendix, page 71).

5. Assess student work by recording the sample number that it most closely matches. Provide one or two reasons for this match.

6. Before giving assessment sheets to students, record student performances using the sample numbers that their work most closely matches.

Figure 13b

Criteria for *group work*	Performance Rubric		
	3	**2**	**1**
– Get along	enjoyed working together as a team	*got along well*	most got along with other group members
– Share ideas	everyone contributed	*most contributed (some more than others)*	some contributed (others needed to be asked)
– Listen to others	all members felt listened to	*most group members listened to others*	some members needed reminders to listen
– Finish the job	completed all work on time (and thoroughly)	got the job done (may have rushed on parts)	*needed more time to finish*
– Use voices that don't bother others	consistently used quiet voices	*reasonably quiet most of the time*	attempted to use quiet voices (needed reminders)

Conference requested ☐

Date(s) received: *Oct. 11*

Assessed by ☑ teacher
☐ self
☐ partner
☐ other

Question(s): *What one thing would your group need to do differently next time to get the job done?*

Assignment: *Group work on poetry unit*

Student: *Deanna L., Lance S., Mary W.*

Figure 14: Performance rubric

PERFORMANCE RUBRIC

With this approach, the focus is on providing a range of descriptions of student performance, written in student language. This way, each individual can see where he or she fits in the overall picture and what he or she needs to work on next. It provides a frame of reference so students can see where they fit in the range and set realistic goals. The most important aspect of this approach is that students can clearly see a range of performance—they may do well on some criteria and not as well on others. From this, they obtain specific information about where and how they can improve.

1. Develop three levels of performance that describe student work. These should relate directly to the criteria that have been set for the project. Write these descriptions on a rubric, such as the one illustrated opposite (or copy the reproducible in the appendix, page 72).

2. Make a copy of this filled-in rubric for each student. Give students a copy so they know the levels of criteria on which they will be assessed.

3. Have students return copies of the rubric to you when they hand in or present their assignments. With a colored highlighter, assess students' performance by highlighting the box for each criterion that most closely matches the work that they have done.

4. Before returning rubrics to students, record student performance. Record the number code that corresponds to your assessment of performance in relation to each of the criteria. (For example, a series of five criteria in a project might be coded 2-1-3-3-3.) Remind students that the numbers are symbols that represent different places on the performance rubric. Their purpose is to give specific feedback that can help students set goals to improve.

Criteria

for *writing a paragraph*	More of	Less of
- uses language effectively	use more of the vocabulary you listed on your web . . . it is powerful	
- provides details to support a main idea	you need more details to fully describe Juliet	
- uses proofreading skills		use fewer commas; check handbook, p. 36
- follows the rules of paragraph writing		

Conference requested ☐	Question(s):
Date(s) received: Nov. 7	
Assessed by ☑ teacher ☐ self ☐ partner ☐ other	Assignment: Descriptive Paragraph Student: Erica S., Block B

Figure 15: More of, Less of

MORE OF, LESS OF

With this approach, students learn where to concentrate their efforts and what aspects of their work count. For example, one student needed to spend more time on research and less time coloring the title page. This approach also shows students that by making a few small changes in one direction or another, they can come closer to meeting the criteria.

1. Make an assessment sheet, such as the one illustrated at left, for each student (or copy the reproducible in the appendix, page 73).

2. Assess student performance by giving students feedback regarding what they have to do more or less of to meet the criteria.

3. Invite students to resubmit their work for the teacher to reassess.

4. Record any comments that you want to remember about the student's work.

N.B. (PAY ATTENTION)

Assessing work in progress is important if we want students to meet with success. The focus of the N.B. approach is on giving students regular, specific feedback about their work while they are in the process of completing it.

Figure 16: N.B. stick-on notes, with criteria they refer to

1. During the progress of an assignment, record on dated stick-on notes what criteria the student needs to pay attention to, and attach them to the work.

2. When students hand in their work, mark notes with a check (✓) or an X indicating whether or not they have paid attention to the "N.B." Transfer the stick-on notes into your records (see figure 22b, page 61).

Criteria for Research

– *generate questions and find sources*

– *collect, record and summarize key information*

– *communicate what you have learned*

N.B. Jan. 16
You will need to use more sources to find the answer to your question... the encyclopedia does not have all the info.

N.B. Jan. 17
Before you go any further, change your topic "Spain" into a question so you know what to focus on.

N.B. Jan. 20
People need to know the sources you've used for your information. Have you kept this list?

N.B. Latin "nota bene," which means "take note" or "pay attention"

Criteria

for *writing a paragraph*   **Specific remarks**

- *uses language effectively*	*your use of transition words (next, after, then) makes it easy to follow*
- *provides detail to support the main ideas*	
- *follows the rules of paragraph writing*	*bring your thoughts to a conclusion by adding a final sentence*
- *uses proofreading skills*	*using the spellcheck program worked — there's not a single error!*

Conference requested ☐

Date(s) received: *Nov. 30*

Assessed by ☑ teacher
☐ self
☐ partner
☐ other

Question(s):

Assignment: *Paragraph*

Student: *Janet K., Block C*

Figure 17: Specific remarks

SPECIFIC REMARKS

Teacher-approval phrases, such as "I like it; this is great," do not provide the information or direction that students need to achieve success. With this approach, the focus is on providing feedback for students that is *specific* and *descriptive*. Students can then repeat a success and will know what they need to improve.

1. Make an assessment sheet, such as the one illustrated opposite, for each student (or copy the reproducible in the appendix, page 74).

2. Assess student performance by giving specific feedback. Describe the performance rather than giving judgments or opinions. For example, a specific remark about a business letter that has "clear statement of purpose" as one of the criteria would be "Your letter clearly indicates dissatisfaction with the product (purpose)." Responding only with a judgment, such as "Good job," provides no way for the students to know what was good and what they should repeat for another time.

3. Before giving the assessment sheets to students, record any remarks that you want to remember about their work.

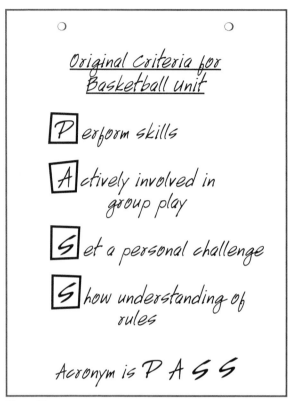

_Original Criteria for
Basketball Unit_

$\boxed{P}$ erform skills

$\boxed{A}$ ctively involved in
group play

$\boxed{S}$ et a personal challenge

$\boxed{S}$ how understanding of
rules

Acronym is $P\ A\ S\ S$

Figure 18a

USING ACRONYMS

Using an acronym helps students remember the criteria. This simple approach also shows that learning is a process, and that we don't necessarily get everything done the first time (nor do we expect to).

1. Examine the criteria to find key words that can be worked into an acronym (see figure 18a, left).

2. Post the acronym on chart paper or the blackboard for students to refer to.

3. Assess student performance by recording the letter(s) of the acronym (criteria) that students have met (see figure 18b, opposite). This immediate feedback lets students know what criteria they have met—and what they still need to work on.

4. Before returning assignments, record the letter(s) of the acronym that students received.

Figure 18: a) Key-word acronym; b) Key-word acronym and assessment stick-on notes. Note in the examples shown below that students might receive only part of the acronym when they first begin a new task (e.g., *ROW*, *BW*).

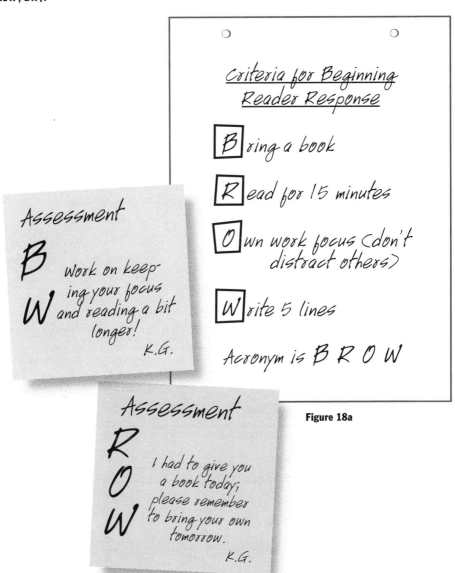

Figure 18a

Figure 18b

Criteria

for *for oral presentation*   **The next step is...**

- *interesting to an audience*	*listen to the audiotape of the presentations and listen to the class enjoying your talk*
- *easy to follow and understand*	*make a chart so the audience can see what you are talking about*
- *speech and manner help audience listen*	*use your cards to prompt you so you don't lose your place*

Conference requested ☐   Question(s):

Date(s) received: *Feb. 10*

Assessed by ☑ teacher   Assignment: *Oral Presentation,*
       ☐ self   *Population Growth in Japan*
       ☐ partner   Student:
       ☐ other   *Simon L., Block C*

Figure 19: The next step

THE NEXT STEP

This approach focuses on showing students how they can take small steps to move forward in their learning when large leaps seem overwhelming.

1. Make an assessment sheet, such as the one illustrated opposite, for each student (or copy the reproducible in the appendix, page 75).

2. Assess student performance by recording two or three steps that they could take to move forward. These could describe some of the ways to improve their work, such as extending ideas, revising specific aspects of the work, and practicing new skills—for example, "Next step: Practice *er* verbs, referring to page 25 in your text" or "Next step: Publish this piece. It is worth it."

3. Before giving assessment sheets back to students, record any "next steps" that you want to remember about their learning.

KEY QUESTIONS

This approach focuses on giving students information that builds on their strengths, points out one or two concerns (maximum of two), and gives suggestions for realistic goals.

1. Make an assessment sheet, such as figure 20 illustrated opposite, for each student (or copy the reproducible in the appendix, page 76).

2. Assess student performance by recording answers to the following key questions: What's working? What's not? What's next?

3. Refer to the criteria that you have shared with your students for specifics to use in your comments.

4. Give students information about what is working so that they have something to build on.

5. Before giving assessment sheets to students, record any points that you want to remember about their learning.

Criteria			
for *problem solving*	**What's working?**	**What's not?**	**What's next?**
- understand the problem	You knew what to look for		
- choose a strategy that works	You tried drawing diagrams and underlining important words		Think back to the problems we did on p. 11 or go talk to Jeremy
- find a correct solution and tell how you got it		You didn't go quite far enough. There's one more step.	
- give examples of this kind of problem outside the classroom	Your example was accurate		

Conference requested ☐   Question(s):

Date(s) received: *May 10*

Assessed by ☑ teacher
          ☐ self
          ☐ partner
          ☐ other

Assignment: *math problem solving, p. 17*

Student: *Anabel G., Block A*

Figure 20: Key questions

3. Questions and Responses

Q. What happens to grades when we use these approaches?

R. In the past, we arrived at grades by totaling the grades and finding percentages. Now we arrive at report card grades using a combination of grades, percentages, notes and observations, and criterion-referenced assessment (which includes scaled scores, symbols, and specific comments).

The criterion-referenced assessment and evaluation process requires us to view a student's performance in relation to what needs to be learned and to the established criteria for evidence of learning, rather than to the performances of other students. We now find that the process of grading involves matching data with descriptions of success or quality rather than totaling and averaging numbers. For us, it means changing the question from "What score or percentage will students need for an A?" to "Which letter-grade description do student performances most closely match?"

We begin by writing a description of what A-level or "Excellent Performance" looks like in our subject area. Sometimes, we write by ourselves; sometimes, we work with colleagues in our department. We write a description for each of the grades A, B, and C.

Then, we help students understand what they need to do to receive an A by showing them the description of "Excellent Performance" and discussing what that means. For example, in an English class, we presented the requirements shown in figure 21a for "Excellent Performance" or A. We then talked with students about the evidence that we would be collecting (see figure 21b).

When it comes time to assign letter grades, we use the following process:

1. Review the assessment data of the student.

2. Look at the descriptions of the letter grades. Highlight the specific phrases in the descriptions that most closely match the student's work.

3. Look for overall patterns of performance and assign the letter grade.

Excellent Performance for English
Requirements for an A

• Reads a great deal of challenging material, often of complex style and form, at an independent level

• Uses a wide variety of strategies to deal with different genres and understands material at both literal and inferential levels

• Responds with a deep and insightful understanding making powerful connections to his or her own life, lives of others, and to other texts

• Writes effectively on a range of topics using complex styles and different forms for a variety of audiences

• Writing consistently follows the rules and conventions (spelling, punctuation, and sentence structure)

• Works productively in groups, and as a part of the class

• Assessments consistently show depth of understanding

Figure 21: a) Sample description of letter grade, above; b) Description of letter grade, with evidence, opposite

Excellent Performance for English
Requirements for an A

- Reads a great deal of challenging material, often of complex style and form, at an independent level
  Evidence: reader response journal including list of books read

- Uses a wide variety of strategies to deal with different genres and understands material at both literal and inferential levels
  Evidence: conferences, test scores, reader response journal

- Responds with a deep and insightful understanding making powerful connections to his or her own life, lives of others, and to other texts
  Evidence: reader response journal, observation, self-assessments

- Writes effectively on a range of topics using complex styles and different forms for a variety of audiences
  Evidence: writing portfolio

- Writing consistently follows the rules and conventions (spelling, punctuation, and sentence structure)
  Evidence: writing portfolio, test scores, project assessments

- Works productively in groups, and as a part of the class
  Evidence: teacher, self and peer assessments, oral presentations

- Assessments consistently show depth of understanding
  Evidence: test scores, project assessments, observations and assignment grades

Figure 21b

Not all of our students' assessments fit neatly into one set of descriptions. By using a highlighter or checking off the phrases in each description that do match, we can point out to our students those aspects of their performance that are considered very good, those that are excellent, and those they need to work on to achieve a particular letter grade.

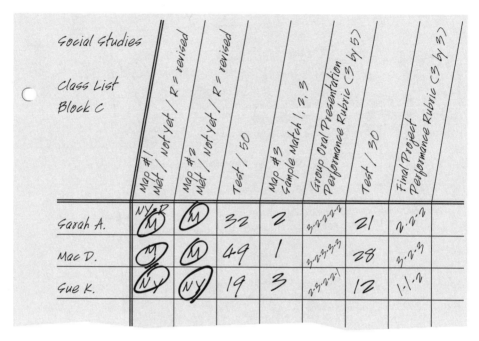

Figure 22: Sample record keeping pages a), above, and b), opposite

Q. How did our record keeping change when we used criteria?

R. Our records now contain more than grades whether in print or digital form. We have one section where we quickly record numbers and symbols (see figure 22a above). We have another part where we record our observations and notes about individual students (see figure 22b, opposite). Some teachers organize these class by class or subject by subject. Regardless of how they are organized, it's important to ensure that there is a wide range of evidence of learning.

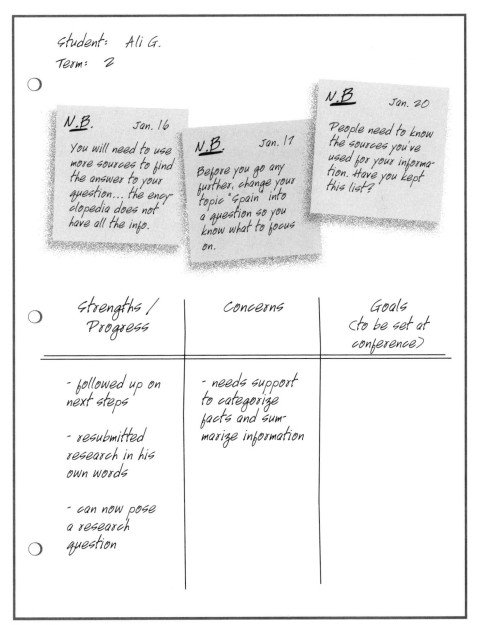

Figure 22b

Q. Can students use these approaches for self-assessment?

R. Yes. The ten assessment approaches described on pages 36–55 can also be used for student self-assessment. We've found that our students need opportunities to discuss the importance of self-assessment and to practice different assessment techniques. Most important, students must know that what they say is being valued and considered by their teacher.

When there is a significant discrepancy between the teacher's and student's own assessments (for example, when the teacher gives an assessment that contradicts a student's self-assessment), students may say, "Why bother doing this? He just does what he wants anyway." Rather than ignoring and negating the student's self-assessment, we ask for a conference. The *only* thing recorded on the assessment sheet is a check (✓) in the conference box.

A conference provides an opportunity for the teacher and students to talk, to look at evidence, and to discuss issues that can never be recorded on a sheet of paper. A student's response to a teacher's questions can add information that the teacher may be unaware of and can clarify points of disagreement. A conference gives both teachers and students an opportunity to clear up any areas of confusion.

For more on student self-assessment, see book 2 of this series, *Self-Assessment and Goal Setting*.

Q. What about the students who cannot meet all the criteria?

R. There may be individuals in our classroom whose needs are so specific that they will not be able to meet all the criteria. We begin by having some students work on meeting one criterion at a time. They start with the criteria they are most familiar with, and we add other criteria as appropriate.

Q. How can I convince my students that they can live without grades?

R. Before we stopped using grades as the only way to assess assignments and projects, we talked with our students about what we would be assessing, and why we would be assessing without grades. We started small, using a single and straightforward way of assessing (for example, Met and Not Yet Met), and stayed with that approach for several weeks or months—whatever it took to have students understand. When they became familiar with one approach, we would move to another, more complex one. We encouraged our students by showing them how they were improving, and by pointing out that they were aware—and could talk about—their own strengths, areas needing improvement, and goals.

We found that our students could live without grades if we developed the criteria for assignments together and made explicit the requirements for success. We provided specific feedback by using assessment approaches that focused on how they were meeting the criteria. The types of assessment we chose to use with students kept their learning in the forefront.

Some of our students still see grades as the currency of school. We realize that for years they have heard, "This part is important. It will be on the test. Learn it to get an A." Now our challenge is to help students become more actively involved in the assessment process. Through this involvement, we have seen many of our students move away from their over-reliance on grades and begin to understand that a single grade cannot possibly communicate the scope and depth of their learning.

Conclusion

Setting and Using Criteria is the first book in the *Knowing What Counts* series—a series that focuses on how to involve students in the process of assessment and evaluation. When we set criteria for assignments, we establish what counts. When we involve students in setting the criteria, we increase their understanding and ownership. When we assess students' work in relation to the criteria without using numbers, we keep the focus on learning. Assessing and evaluating in ways that support the learning of all our students is what counts for us.

Appendix: Reproducibles

Note: The following pages may be reproduced for classroom use. To enlarge to 8½" x 11" (21.5 cm x 28 cm), please set photocopier at 143 percent, and align top edge of page with corresponding edge of copier glass.

Criteria

for	Met	Not yet met

Conference requested ☐

Date(s) received:

Assessed by ☐ teacher
          ☐ self
          ☐ partner
          ☐ other

Question(s):

Assignment:

Student:

Setting and Using Criteria, 2nd Edition, by K. Gregory, C. Cameron, and A. Davies
© 1997, 2011 · solution-tree.com

Criteria

for	Met	Not yet met	I noticed ...

Conference requested ☐

Question(s):

Date(s) received:

Assessed by ☐ teacher
           ☐ self
           ☐ partner
           ☐ other

Assignment:

Student:

Criteria
for

Sample Match
Closest match is sample #_____ because ...

Conference requested ☐

Date(s) received:

Assessed by ☐ teacher
         ☐ self
         ☐ partner
         ☐ other

Question(s):

Assignment:

Student:

Criteria

for

Performance Rubric

	3	2	1

Conference requested ☐

Question(s):

Date(s) received:

Assessed by ☐ teacher
☐ self
☐ partner
☐ other

Assignment:

Student:

Setting and Using Criteria, 2nd Edition, by K. Gregory, C. Cameron, and A. Davies
© 1997, 2011 · solution-tree.com

Criteria

for	More of	Less of

Conference requested ☐

Question(s):

Date(s) received:

Assessed by ☐ teacher
         ☐ self
         ☐ partner
         ☐ other

Assignment:

Student:

Setting and Using Criteria, 2nd Edition, by K. Gregory, C. Cameron, and A. Davies
© 1997, 2011 · solution-tree.com

Criteria

for **Specific remarks**

Conference requested ☐

Date(s) received:

Assessed by ☐ teacher
☐ self
☐ partner
☐ other

Question(s):

Assignment:

Student:

Setting and Using Criteria, 2nd Edition, by K. Gregory, C. Cameron, and A. Davies
© 1997, 2011 · solution-tree.com

Criteria

for

The next step is...

Conference requested ☐

Question(s):

Date(s) received:

Assessed by ☐ teacher
☐ self
☐ partner
☐ other

Assignment:

Student:

Criteria

for	What's working?	What's not?	What's next?

Conference requested ☐

Question(s):

Date(s) received:

Assessed by ☐ teacher
             ☐ self
             ☐ partner
             ☐ other

Assignment:

Student:

Bibliography

Anthony, R., T. Johnson, N. Mickelson, & A. Preece. 1991. *Evaluating Literacy: A Perspective for Change.* Portsmouth, NH: Heinemann.

Caine, R. & G. Caine. 1991. *Making Connections: Teaching and the Human Brain.* Alexandria, VA: Association for Supervision and Curriculum Development.

Davies, A., C. Cameron, C. Politano, & K. Gregory. 1992. *Together Is Better: Collaborative Assessment, Evaluation, and Reporting.* Winnipeg, MB: Peguis.

Kohn, A. 1993. *Punished by Rewards.* New York: Houghton Mifflin.

Stiggins, R. 1996. *Student-Centered Classroom Assessment.* 2nd Ed. New York: Merrill.

Kathleen Gregory, BA, MEd, has more than 30 years' experience teaching at secondary, elementary, and middle schools. With a background in assessment practices and literacy strategies, she has also been a district curriculum coordinator and a support teacher for classroom teachers and school teams who are integrating students with special needs. A former teacher-in-residence at the University of Victoria, Kathleen is currently an instructor for literacy and assessment courses for preservice teachers and is a consultant to many school districts in developing their own approaches to conferencing, reporting, and authentic assessment strategies.

Caren Cameron, MEd, has worked as a teacher, a District Principal of Educational Programs, and a sessional instructor at the University of Victoria. Currently she is an educational consultant working with school districts across Canada on a variety of topics including assessment and leadership. She is the co-author of a dozen practical books for colleagues, including a series for middle and primary years called *Voices of Experience*.

Anne Davies, PhD, is a researcher, writer, and consultant. She has been a teacher, school administrator, and system leader, and has taught at universities in Canada and the United States. She is a published author of more than 30 books and multimedia resources, as well as numerous chapters and articles. She is author or co-author of the best-selling books *Making Classroom Assessment Work*, the *Knowing What Counts* series and the *Leaders Series*. A recipient of the Hilroy Fellowship for Innovative Teaching, Anne continues to support others to learn more about assessment in the service of learning and learners.